Children's Multicultural & Character Education Book Series

Finders Keepers?

A Bus Trip in India

Robert Arnett
Illustrated by Smita Turakhia

Atman Press

Text © 2017 by Robert Arnett
Illustrations © 2017 by Smita Turakhia

Editors: Smita Turakhia, Doug Glener
Map: Scott McIntyre

Published in the United States of America by
Atman Press
2104 Cherokee Avenue,
 Columbus, Georgia 31906-1424
AtmanPress@gmail.com
www.AtmanPress.com

Third Edition—2017
Printed by Create Space, An Amazon.Com Company
Finders Keepers? is also published in Spanish
under the title ¿Es mío?

Summary: Text and illustrations introduce the
traditions, daily life, and values of the people of India.
Emphasizes important universal values for children.
Includes glossary, pronunciations of Indian words,
and craft activity.

ISBN: 978-1-946833-00-6

A Special Gift For:

_____

From:

_____

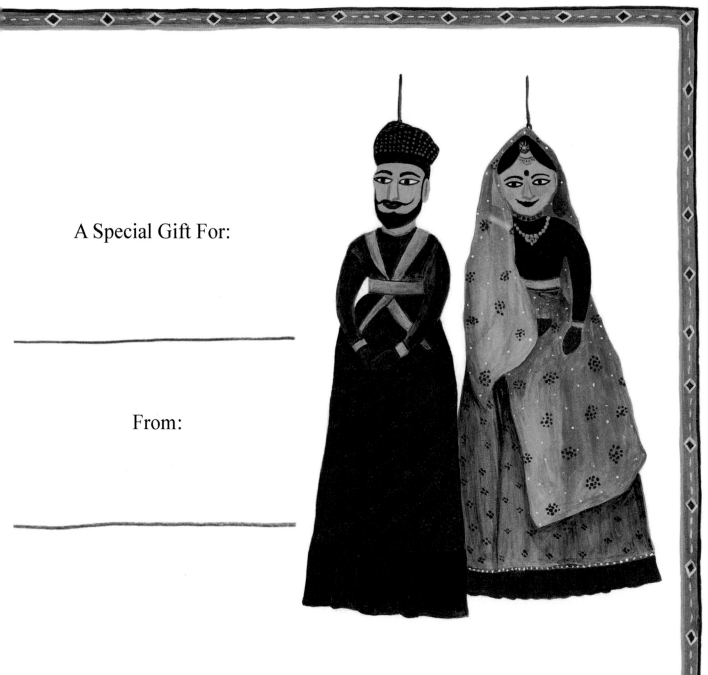

This book is dedicated to the silent voice within each of us that prompts us to do what is right.

A Warm Welcome

In India, a toran (TOH-run) is hung over a doorway as a sign of welcome. Torans made of fresh flowers and leaves can be seen all across the country.

In the state of Rajasthan (RAH-juh-stahn) in northwest India where this story takes place, torans are made of fabric and often decorated with brightly colored embroidery, appliqués, and mirrors. The cloth pennants that hang down from torans represent leaves from sacred trees.

This toran welcomes you to *Finders Keepers?*. As you turn these pages, may you enjoy traveling with me to India.

It is hard to look out a window and see the sights of the Indian countryside when every time your bus goes over a bump, you bounce so high off your seat you almost hit your head on the roof!

But there I was, bouncing along on my way to Mt. Abu (Mount AH-boo), a small town on a mountain in the state of Rajasthan.

Some adventurous men and boys who could not get seats inside the bus rode on top with the luggage.

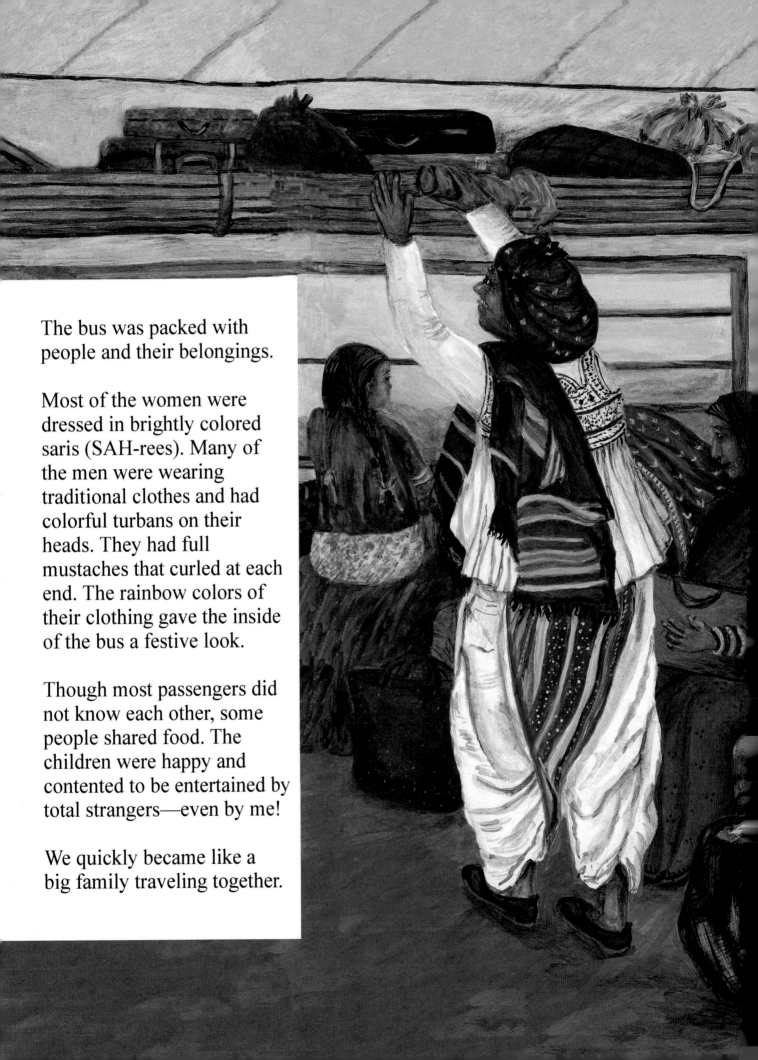

The bus was packed with people and their belongings.

Most of the women were dressed in brightly colored saris (SAH-rees). Many of the men were wearing traditional clothes and had colorful turbans on their heads. They had full mustaches that curled at each end. The rainbow colors of their clothing gave the inside of the bus a festive look.

Though most passengers did not know each other, some people shared food. The children were happy and contented to be entertained by total strangers—even by me!

We quickly became like a big family traveling together.

How beautiful to look upon everyone you meet as part of your family

and being as dear to you
as a brother, a sister,
or a parent.

As our bus continued along the winding mountain road, I could see an old fort on top of a steep hill. Its tall, massive walls must have made it difficult to conquer.

Throughout history, the people of Rajasthan have been admired for their bravery, sense of honor, loyalty, and love of freedom.

Even when invading armies much larger than theirs attacked the cities of Rajasthan, the townspeople would seldom surrender and often would fight to the last man. The women of Rajasthan were equally brave.

The stories of their heroic deeds are often painted on walls of homes and palaces.

We stopped for lunch at a roadside rest stop. As I got off the bus,
I saw several people pointing up at a tree.

I was amazed to see large bats hanging upside down from the
tree limbs, roosting during the day. The harmless fruit bats, called
flying foxes, looked like special effects from a movie.

At a nearby food stall, a man was boiling milk mixed with sugar in a large cauldron over an open fire. I bought a glass of hot milk that he topped with some cream skimmed from the surface of the steaming liquid.

To cool it for me, a boy skillfully poured it from one glass to another.

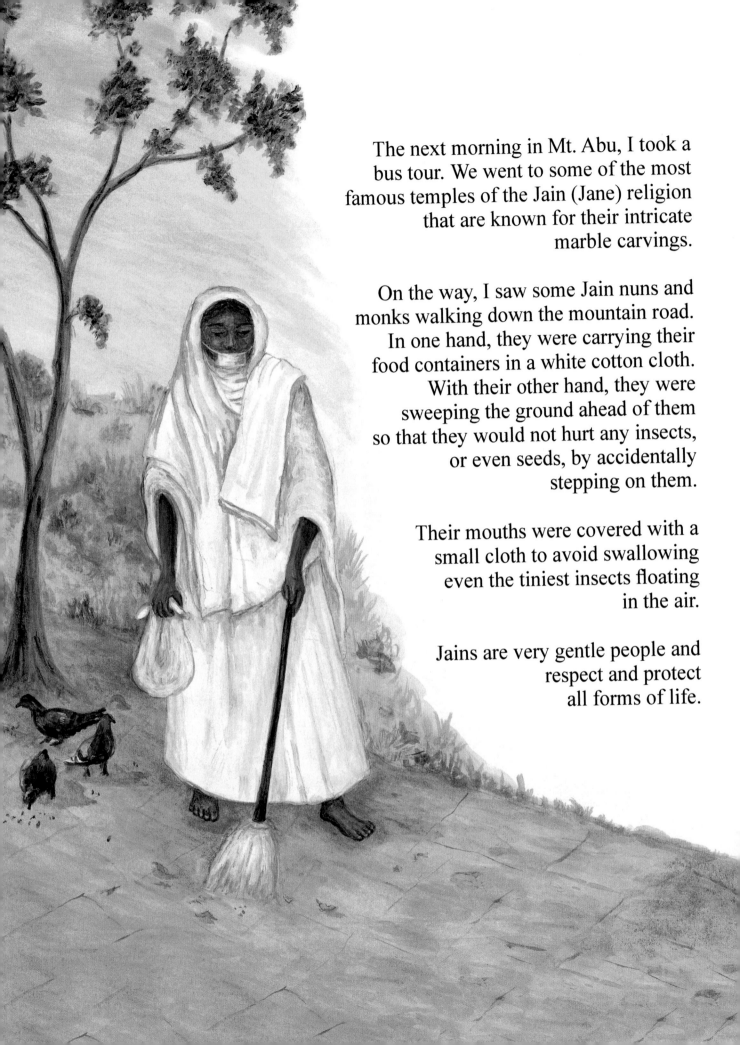

The next morning in Mt. Abu, I took a bus tour. We went to some of the most famous temples of the Jain (Jane) religion that are known for their intricate marble carvings.

On the way, I saw some Jain nuns and monks walking down the mountain road. In one hand, they were carrying their food containers in a white cotton cloth. With their other hand, they were sweeping the ground ahead of them so that they would not hurt any insects, or even seeds, by accidentally stepping on them.

Their mouths were covered with a small cloth to avoid swallowing even the tiniest insects floating in the air.

Jains are very gentle people and respect and protect all forms of life.

We also went to a Hindu (HIN-doo) temple that had a statue of the Hindu deity Shiva (SHEE-vah) in a symbolic dancing pose.

To Hindus, Shiva represents God's power that brings all things into creation and takes everything back to its origin when its stay in the world is completed.

Though Hinduism believes in only one God, it gives Him many names and forms. The statues serve as symbols. They help people better understand God's numerous functions in the world.

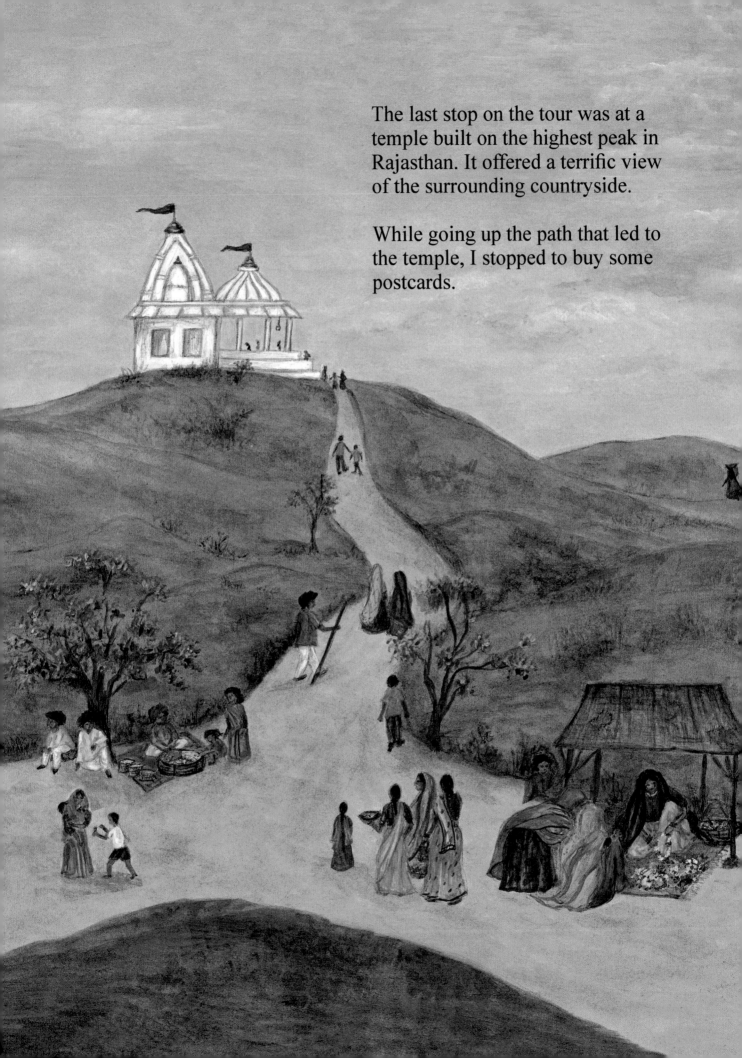

The last stop on the tour was at a temple built on the highest peak in Rajasthan. It offered a terrific view of the surrounding countryside.

While going up the path that led to the temple, I stopped to buy some postcards.

As I walked away, I felt someone tapping my elbow.
A young boy with dark hair was standing behind me.

To my surprise, in his outstretched hand was my wallet.
I must have dropped it when I bought the postcards.

I offered the boy a reward for returning my wallet, but he would not accept it. I even tried to put some money into his hands, but he put them behind his back.

Again, I made an attempt to reward him for his honesty, but he refused. I could not understand why the boy would not take the money.

A man passing by stopped to watch us. He could speak English, so I asked him to help me. "This boy found my wallet and returned it to me. Please explain to him that I want to reward him for his honesty."

The man began talking to the boy in their language. After a few minutes, the boy did most of the talking. I was beginning to wonder if either of them understood me.

Then the man turned to me and said, "This boy does not understand why you should give him any money for returning to you what is yours. The idea of accepting a reward for doing the right thing makes no sense to him."

Finders keepers? No way!

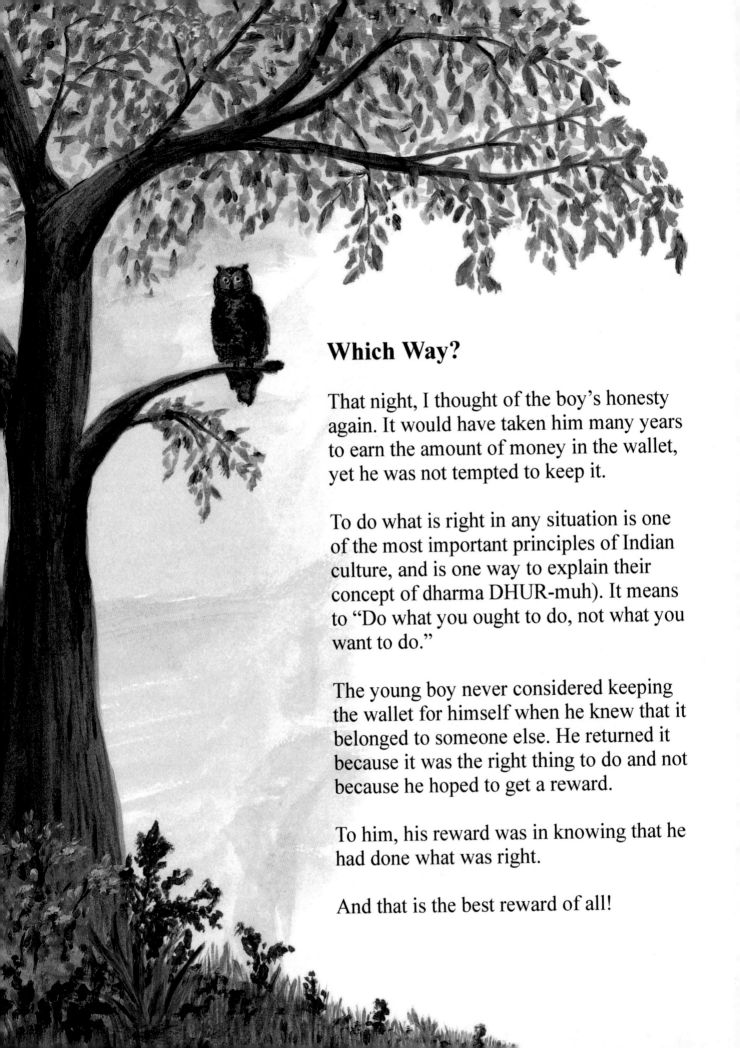

Which Way?

That night, I thought of the boy's honesty again. It would have taken him many years to earn the amount of money in the wallet, yet he was not tempted to keep it.

To do what is right in any situation is one of the most important principles of Indian culture, and is one way to explain their concept of dharma DHUR-muh). It means to "Do what you ought to do, not what you want to do."

The young boy never considered keeping the wallet for himself when he knew that it belonged to someone else. He returned it because it was the right thing to do and not because he hoped to get a reward.

To him, his reward was in knowing that he had done what was right.

And that is the best reward of all!

Now it is time for me to say "*Namaste*" (NUM-ah-stay). "*Namaste*" is how many Indians greet each other instead of saying "hello" and "goodbye."

While uttering "*namaste*," they place the fingers and palms of both hands together in front of the chest and slightly bow the head. It is also called a *pranam* (pruh-NAHM) and is a gesture of humility and respect.

In the ancient Sanskrit (SAN-skrit) language, to *pranam*, or to say *namaste*, means "my soul bows to your soul."

Namaste expresses the belief that God is present deep within each person, that skin color, race, or religion does not alter the soul-image of God within each of us.

Life is a journey.

Let your inner voice
be your guide.

Treat all who cross
your path with love
and kindness.

Gallantly, reach for
the stars.

"Namaste!"

Let's Make a Paper Toran

Materials:
- 6" x 18" strip of green construction paper, or any bright color
- 12" x 18" yellow construction paper, or any bright color
- scraps of brightly colored fabric, or colored paper
- 8-12 small round mirrors, or clear rhinestones from craft store
- 25" piece of string or yarn
- white craft glue
- red masking tape, or any bright color
- scissors
- patterns from this page

Follow the Steps:

1. Using the pattern cut 4 to 6 pennants from yellow construction paper.

2. Cut scraps of brightly colored fabric or paper into small squares and triangles.

3. Glue the cut squares, triangles, and rhinestones to the 4 yellow pennants to form designs.

4. Repeat step 3 on the long 6" x 18" strip of green construction paper.

5. Turn the 4 yellow pennants and the 6" x 18" strip of green construction paper so the design is face down. Glue the 4 yellow pennants to the bottom edge of the green strip. Glue the string horizontally across the top edge of the green strip. Let dry.

6. Turn the glued parts from step 5 face up. Tape colored masking tape horizontally across the green strip where the pennants are attached.

7. Loop both ends of the string.

8. Hang the toran over a doorway to give your guests a warm welcome.

Food For Thought

Think of the young boy. His good deed proved that he did not need anyone to tell him the right thing to do. He listened to his conscience.

The dictionary defines conscience as the recognition within us of right and wrong regarding what we do and why we do it. It urges us towards right action.

Some people believe that our conscience, or inner voice, is the silent voice of God trying to guide us and that if we listen to it, we will always do what is right.

◆ Would you do something just to please someone else when your inner voice says it is wrong?

When we do the right thing, we feel so good about ourselves that we do not need to seek the approval of our friends.

◆ Do you think you should be paid to help around the house for doing things like keeping your room clean or washing the dishes?

◾ Is it not your responsibility as a part of the family to help with the chores at home?

People around the world do things in many different ways.

- What is your favorite ice cream flavor? Do you know someone whose favorite flavor is different from yours?

- Which of the two flavors tastes better? Is it possible that their favorite flavor tastes as good to them as your favorite flavor tastes to you?

Not all people think in the same way. Try to understand their way of thinking, even if it is different from yours.

In order to get along better with others, practice looking at things from their viewpoint, and keep an open mind. They may be right, too, and you might learn something new!

Jog Your Memory

◈ *dharma* (DHUR-muh)
In Hinduism it means to do what is right, regardless of the circumstances.

◈ **Hinduism**
The largest religion of India. It is one of the oldest religions in the world.

◈ **Jains** (Janes)
Followers of Jainism. Their religion began in India over 2,500 years ago.

◈ *pranam* (pruh-NAHM)
A custom of placing both hands together in front of one's chest and bowing the head when greeting someone with *namaste*.

◈ **sari** (SAH-ree)
An 18-foot-long cloth worn by women that wraps around the waist to form a skirt and then drapes over the shoulder. It is worn with a tight fitting blouse.

◈ **Hindu** (HIN-doo)
A follower of Hinduism. Hindus believe in only one God, but give God many forms to make it easier to understand His role in the world.

◈ **humility**
Not seeing oneself as being more important or being better than others.

◈ *namaste* (NUM-ah-stay)
Hindu greeting for "hello" and "goodbye." It means "my soul bows to your soul."

◈ **Sanskrit** (SAN-skrit)
The religious and literary language of ancient India. Sanskrit is the oldest surviving language in the world.

◈ **Shiva** (SHEE-vah)
Hindu deity who represents God's power that brings all things into creation and takes everything back to its origin when its stay in creation is completed.

turban
A cloth wrapped around the head to form a headdress for men.

toran (TOH-run)
A hanging used over a doorway in India as a sign of welcome. It is believed to bring good luck.

Did You Know?

India is one of the oldest civilizations in the world.

India is the largest democracy in the world.

India has the second largest number of people in the world.

In India, going from one state to another can be like traveling to another country. Its customs, celebrations, foods, and even languages are very different from one another.

India has over 1,650 languages that are considered mother tongues, the language spoken in a person's home.

Most students learn to speak three languages in school: English, Hindi, and the language spoken in their own state.

Algebra, calculus, and trigonometry were invented in India.

The number system, the number zero, and the decimal system were developed in India over 1,500 years ago.

Brain surgeries and other advanced operations were performed in India over 2,500 years ago.

The Author

Robert Arnett was inspired to write *Finders Keepers?* by the high ideals of a young boy he encountered in a small town in India.

A native of Columbus, Georgia, Arnett has traveled throughout much of the world and developed a deep appreciation and respect for world cultures. He has made six trips to India that totaled almost two years, during which he traveled the length and breadth of the country studying art, culture, and religion while living with Indian families.

He is the author and photographer of the internationally acclaimed book *India Unveiled: Spirit, Tradition, People*, a travelogue illustrated with award-winning photography, which has won numerous distinguished awards.

Arnett has spoken widely throughout North America, including the Smithsonian Institution, The Kennedy Center, Harvard, Yale, MIT, and Stanford Universities. He has also given numerous presentations at schools, libraries, community organizations, temples, and churches. He has been interviewed on National Public Radio, Voice of America, and various television programs.

For more information about Robert Arnett's books or to arrange a presentation in your city, visit www.AtmanPress.com or you may email him at AtmanPress@gmail.com.

The Illustrator

The paintings in *Finders Keepers?* come from the hand and heart of Smita Turakhia, a children's illustrator who paints mainly from inspiration and the desire to share the best of India's culture with children. She was a featured illustrator at The Kennedy Center and has given presentations at the Smithsonian Institution, book festivals, and many schools and libraries. Her portfolio includes illustrations for *The Journey to the Truth*, an award-winning DVD that depicted the messages and metaphors of the Bhagavad Gita in the Warli folk art style of India. She is also the editor and associate photographer for *India Unveiled: Spirit, Tradition, People* by Robert Arnett.

Turakhia was born and grew up in Mumbai, India, where she graduated from Nirmala Niketan. While traveling in the United States with her father, he intimated to her that he would like for her to do something meaningful with her artistic talents. After she moved to the United States, she studied fine arts for two years at the University of New Mexico, Albuquerque. Now, besides fulfilling her father's vision, she is living her own dreams of bringing India's cultural heritage to life through art.

Turakhia resides in Texas with her husband. You may contact her at SmitaTurakhia@gmail.com.

Made in the USA
San Bernardino, CA
02 June 2020